Forever His

31 Musings from a Heart in Love with God

Otescia R. Johnson

Scripture quotations marked (AMP) are taken from the Amplified Bible, Copyright © 2015 by The Lockman Foundation. Used by permission. lockman.org

Scripture quotations marked (NLT) are taken from the Holy Bible, New Living Translation, copyright ©1996, 2004, 2015 by Tyndale House Foundation. Used by permission of Tyndale House Publishers, Carol Stream, Illinois 60188. All rights reserved.

Scripture quotations marked MSG are taken from The Message, copyright © 1993, 2002, 2018 by Eugene H. Peterson. Used by permission of NavPress. All rights reserved. Represented by Tyndale House Publishers.

Scripture quotations marked TPT are from The Passion Translation®. Copyright © 2017, 2018, 2020 by Passion & Fire Ministries, Inc. Used by permission. All rights reserved. ThePassionTranslation.com.

FOREVER HIS.

Copyright © 2024 All rights reserved—Otescia R. Johnson

No part of this book may be reproduced or transmitted in any form or by any means, graphic, electronic, or mechanical, including photocopying, recording, taping, or by an information storage retrieval system without the written permission of the publisher. The contents and cover of this book may not be reproduced in whole or in part in any form without the express written permission of the author or B.O.Y. Enterprises, Inc.

Please direct all copyright inquiries to:

B.O.Y. Publications, Inc.
c/o Author Copyrights
P.O. Box 262
Lowell, NC 28098
betonyourselfent.com

Paperback ISBN: 978-1-955605-73-1

Cover and Interior Design: B.O.Y. Enterprises, Inc.

Printed in the United States.

Dedication

For everyone who desires to start a love affair
with the greatest lover ever known.

Table of Contents

A Letter to the Reader 7
You are New 9
I Will Not Labor in Vain 12
Worship 15
What About My Plans? 18
Unconditional Love 23
A Prayer for my children 27
A Surrendered Heart Harkens… 30
I Have an Assurance of Victory! 32
Why do you cry to me? 34
You Are Just the Vessel 38
Know the Members of Your Herd! 41
I Fell in Love in a Closet 44
Worship Part 2 47
A Lifestyle of Prayer and Fasting 49
God's Decree 52
Write Everything He Gives You 55
He desires to give you your heart's desires! 58
Thank You for my Husband 63
Watch YOUR Mouth 66
Think on These Things 70
I Miss My Brother 72
A Loving Father 77
He Leads Me to His Best 79
Worship Part 3 84
Come See a Man 86
The God Who Reads My Tears 93

Prayer for My Sons 96
For your Maker is Your Husband... 100
The Lord is My Provider... 103
My heart safely trusts in God... 107
A Poem from my Dreams.. 110
More books by Otescia R. Johnson... 113

Otescia R. Johnson

A Letter to the Reader

The devotional you are about to read was released on October 11, 2024, my 43rd birthday, which happened to be a Friday. Typically, I would not release a book on Friday as it is industry standard to release new books on Tuesdays. However, I felt a very strong nudge from God to compile and release this devotional, on my birthday. I had no plans to release a book this year, yet the gentle nudge came to finish this project I'd started and set aside years ago. Then, as it neared completion, I was urged to look up the number 43 in my concordance. I started by searching H43 to discover where the Hebrew word represented by this number was used in scripture. It led me to the name Ebiasaph which means "my father has gathered". Next, I progressed to the New Testament and searched G43 which led me to a word that is translated as "arm". This word is used biblically to mean "anything closely enfolding".

As the revelation of these terms settled within in me, I heard the phrase, "My father has gathered and closely enfolded me." This is a perfect example of the relationship I have with our Heavenly Father. I lavish my love upon Him through obedience to His word and time in His presence, and He in turn lavishes His love upon me. Over the years, as I have become more and more intentional about deepening my relationship with Him, He has responded by engulfing me in His unfailing love.

This devotional is a collection of letters, blog entries, prayers, thoughts, songs, and questions that I've mused on as my relationship with God has grown. My prayer, in sharing something so deeply personal, is that readers will feel a nudge to also deepen their relationship with the Father. No matter what life throws your way, know that He is right there to guide, comfort, and love you through it all.

Song of Songs 6:3 says, "I am my beloved's, and my beloved is mine…" which sums up the theme of this book. I am able to honestly say my heart is in love with God because He has revealed the depth of His love for me. This is a relationship that has revealed God to me as a Father, Friend, Confidant, Provider, Restorer, Rescuer, Redeemer, Teacher, and the lover of my soul. It is the most rewarding and fulfilling relationship any human can ever experience.

As you take a peek into what I am honored to experience with God, I pray your relationship with Him grows to depths you never imagined.

From my heart to yours,

Otescia

Day 1
You are New

"This means that anyone who belongs to Christ has become a new person. The old life is gone; a new life has begun! And all of this is a gift from God, who brought us back to himself through Christ. And God has given us this task of reconciling people to him. For God was in Christ, reconciling the world to himself, no longer counting people's sins against them. And he gave us this wonderful message of reconciliation. So we are Christ's ambassadors; God is making his appeal through us. We speak for Christ when we plead, "Come back to God!" For God made Christ, who never sinned, to be the offering for our sin, so that we could be made right with God through Christ."

-2 Corinthians 5:17-21 NLT

This is a very familiar passage of scripture, but have you ever really sat and thought about what it means to become a new person? This is not like a makeover where clothes, hair, and makeup are changed but the person in the clothes remains the same. In fact, it's the opposite. When the Bible says "become a new person" it literally means you are no longer the person you were before you came into relationship with God. Your old patterns and ways of doing things will shift over time during your process of sanctification. But the moment you accepted Jesus Christ as your Lord and Savior and invited Him to sit on the throne of your heart, the old version of you died and a new version was born.

Take a moment to meditate on 2 Corinthians 5:17-21. What is Holy Spirit saying to you about it? Record your experience below.

_____
_____
_____
_____
_____
_____
_____
_____
_____
_____
_____
_____
_____
_____
_____
_____
_____

Otescia R. Johnson

Day 2
I Will Not Labor in Vain

"If God's grace doesn't help the builders, they will labor in vain to build a house. If God's mercy doesn't protect the city, all the sentries will circle it in vain. It really is senseless to work so hard from early morning till late at night, toiling to make a living for fear of not having enough. God can provide for his devoted lovers even while they sleep!" **-Psalms 127:1-2 TPT**

I can't continue to labor in vain…

That's the thought that came to me when I read this scripture. Attempting to "tough it out" and "power through it" have led me to laboring in vain, which of course, leads to burn out. I don't want to continue in cycles of burnout. I long for the ease of trusting God and following His plan for my life.

The world's way of doing things always leads to stress and hyper-consumption. God's way of doing things leads to rest and supernatural provision. Why then, is it so easy to turn away from God's prescribed design? Why have we subscribed to the world's system of toiling?

When you think about your life and accomplishments, can you honestly say you've allowed the Lord to build your "house", or have you fallen into the exhausting trap of laboring in vain?

Take a moment to review your plans for the remainder of the year, or even next year. Are these plans more of what leads to laboring in vain? What adjustments do you need to make to return to trusting God's design and process for your life?

_____
_____
_____
_____
_____
_____
_____
_____
_____
_____
_____
_____
_____
_____

Forever His

Day 3
Worship

Worship is the mirror whereby which we view the truth of ourselves. I don't know where I first heard this truth, or if I ever heard it. I just know it is a true statement of what I've experienced. When I worship the Father, He lavishes His love upon me, but He also corrects me and shines light into the dark broken places of my heart. It was a moment of worship that truly introduced me to the lover of my soul. It was worship that created the atmosphere and space for God to minister to me regarding forgiveness. It was worship that showed me the error in my ways when I refused to acknowledge my need for help. Worship has led to me apologizing to others as well as myself and repenting to God. Worship has produced books, poems, journal entries, Bible Studies, businesses, programs, and so much more. It is the balm to my soul and the expression of the air that I breathe. Worship has always been the launching pad for transformative conversations with the One who knew me before He formed me in my mother's womb.

Take a moment to find and listen to the song "Thank You" by Victor Thompson. You should be able to find the song on YouTube or other music streaming platforms. It is one of the songs that ushered me into a beautiful time of worship and adoration.

After you listen to the song, take a moment to reflect on what you sense, see, hear, and feel. Use the space below to record your experience.

Otescia R. Johnson

Day 4
What About My Plans?

By nature, I am one who loves to plan everything out. I have been known to spend hours preparing and plotting out courses of action for future success. Previously, I lived by the motto, "to fail to plan is to plan to fail". Oh, how untrue and incorrect this saying is.

Through time spent in fellowship with the Lord, I have learned (through trial and lots of error I might add) that all the natural planning in the world is pointless without the guidance of Holy Spirit. It is very easy to lay out a map to success, but if Jesus is not in the driver's seat there is no guarantee we'll end up at God's desired location. And let's face it, if we are not aiming for God's desired location, then what's the point of the trip?

We often say to God, "Lord, I'll go where you want me to go. I'll do what you want me to do." Well, what if He wants to you to go to a remote country and devote yourself totally to mission work? Are you willing to go? What if He wants you to quit your job and devote yourself to ministering to the homeless? Are you willing to do it?

Are you willing to abandon ALL of your plans for God's plans?

When I was first asked this question, I could not readily answer it. Not because my heart did not want to do the will of the Father, but because I have recently gained a deeper understanding of what that means. It is easy to say yes Lord when we only have a surface level of understanding as to what He is calling for, but what about when we gain a deeper level of understanding? Remember, in all of our getting, we are to get an understanding.

For me, saying "Yes Lord" means laying down my every desire, hope, and dream for the future. It is being willing and able to let go of the home I've dreamed about since I was a teenager, the career that is literally at my fingertips... the "good life" we see here on Earth. It means going to God DAILY and laying those things down. It means turning down opportunities that the Father says turn down. It means moving to a place I had no desire to move to so that He could be glorified through my service. It means serving the people with no hope or expectation of anything in return. It means forgoing my favorite movies and television programs to spend time alone with Him. It means doing the hard things He presses upon my heart to do. It means making the conscience choice to be obedient to the promptings of Holy Spirit. It means literally burying ALL of my plans and asking the Father to impregnate me with His. I am no longer my own. I have been made new by the Father, and it is my prayer that He will continually make me over until I look like Him.

Because my view of the future is limited, I cannot make the BEST decision concerning my future. Me planning my future is like a person attempting to draw a map to a location to which they have never been. God however, in His infinite wisdom is all knowing, and all seeing. He sees what lays ahead, so when He draws the map, He takes me directly to the location He has ordained for my life. When He leads, I will never make a wrong turn, and I will reach His desired location in His perfect timing!

What about my plans? I ripped them up. When I reviewed them in better lighting, I saw mistakes all over the blueprints. They were worthless. I have adopted Heavenly blueprints, and though I can not see or even understand every phase, I know the result will be a beautiful masterpiece for I know the Master's thoughts toward me. He has thoughts of peace towards me, and He desires to give me an expected end! (Jeremiah 29:11)

Use the space below to surrender your plans to the Lord. Then ask Him to reveal His plans for your life and record what you sense, see, hear, and feel.

Forever His

Day 5
Unconditional Love

One of my favorite stories ever told, is the love story I get the joy of living with my husband Lyndell. We met in God's perfect timing when we both chose to trust God with our hearts. In turn, He introduced us to each other and began to reveal Himself to us. I'd never quite recognized how God expresses Himself through people until God used my husband to teach me about unconditional love. While my parents genuinely love me, I always felt like I needed to be better, change something, or live up to their expectations. That's not to discredit their parenting or love for me. It's how I felt based on the way I was filtering my experiences with them. Everyone I'd previously been close to, had a front row seat to my issues and called me out in different ways. Out of my own immaturity, it felt like everyone wanted me to change something about myself to make me worthy of their love. When you have this type of broken understanding of love, it makes it very difficult to accept anyone who claims to love you unconditionally, even God.

When Lyndell came into my life, I slowly revealed pieces of myself to him, afraid that if I showed him all of me, he'd leave or give me an ultimatum about what needed to change. On the one hand, I felt if he was the one, he'd be able to accept all of me. On the other, I was worried that he'd eventually find something that was a deal breaker for him. To try to stay ahead of his potential departure, I'd ask him, "Is there anything you'd like for me to change or do differently?" Thank God for the fruit of patience in my husband because I lost count of the number of times I asked him the same question. Each time he'd answer the same, "I love you just the way you are. I don't want you to change anything."

It took me about a year and a few mistakes for his answer to fully sink in. It did not matter to him that I wasn't perfect. He wanted me as his wife forever because he loved me…all of me… unconditionally. When this thought hit me, I began to weep. I was so shocked because I'd heard people speak of unconditional love, but I didn't think I'd previously experienced it. In that moment, God revealed to me my husband was given to me as a human example of Christ's love for the church and His love for me. God taught me how to recognize and experience unconditional love through the love of my husband.

Knowing God will love me no matter what caused me to finally understand why I love the 8th chapter of the book of Romans so much. In Romans 8:38-39 (TPT), the

Apostle Paul wrote, *"So now I live with the confidence that there is nothing in the universe with the power to separate us from God's love. I'm convinced that his love will triumph over death, life's troubles, fallen angels, or dark rulers in the heavens. There is nothing in our present or future circumstances that can weaken his love. There is no power above us or beneath us—no power that could ever be found in the universe that can distance us from God's passionate love, which is lavished upon us through our Lord Jesus, the Anointed One!"*

God's love for us is an impenetrable force. No sin, distance, or ignorance can separate us from Him or change the way He feels about us. More than anything else, God longs to have all of His children walk in total healing and wholeness as we walk with Him through the journey of life. God wants us all to recognize and enjoy His unfailing love.

As you journal today, think over your life and record the ways God has revealed His unconditional love to you.

_____

_____

_____

_____

_____

Forever His

Day 6
A Prayer for my children

Father God, I come to you as humbly as I know how, thanking you for my life and the very air that I breathe. I praise you for the beauty of your handiwork. All that I have is because of You and your generosity towards me. Thank you for the gift of my children. I pray now Lord, that you would forgive me for all sins I have committed. Holy Spirit, please reveal any hidden sin to me so that I may repent and turn away from it. Thank you, Father, for hearing my prayer of repentance and forgiving me!

Lord, you said in your word in Isaiah 49:25 that You would contend with him that contends with me and You would save my children. God, I lift each of my children up to you now as I stand on Your word as my anchor. I ask that You keep your promise to me concerning their lives and salvation. I ask that You teach me how to connect with each of them and mother them according to their individual needs. And Father, the places I have not been graced to speak to, please send someone who is anchored in You to minister to them. Send people they will be open to listening to so that Your word will penetrate their hearts, minds, and souls. Captivate their hearts Lord so that they will fall in love with you as I have. Draw them close to you by your spirit so that they will have the desire to hide your word within their heart. Lord, you see every blind spot I may have missed, and You love them far more than I'll ever be able to comprehend. Fill in the holes I missed according to your omniscience. Surround my children with your favor and seal their righteousness in You, in Jesus' name, Amen.

Use the space below to write a prayer for your children, grandchildren, or godchildren.

_____
_____
_____
_____
_____
_____
_____
_____
_____
_____

Otescia R. Johnson

Day 7
A Surrendered Heart Harkens...

"Make very sure that you never refuse to listen to God when he speaks! For the God who spoke on earth from Sinai is the same God who now speaks from heaven. Those who heard him speak his living Word on earth found nowhere to hide, so what chance is there for us to escape if we turn our backs on God and refuse to hear his warnings as he speaks from heaven? The earth was rocked at the sound of his voice from the mountain, but now he has promised, "Once and for all I will not only shake the systems of the world, but also the unseen powers in the heavenly realm!" **-Hebrews 12:25-26 (TPT)**

Many people debate on whether or not God is speaking "that much". It seems an odd debate when as Christians, we have based our lives upon the word of God. Yet, we have so many people who profess to follow Christ yet ignore God when He is attempting to speak to them. How can we call ourselves Christians if we don't first do what Christ did, which was listen to the voice of His Father in Heaven?

A surrendered heart harkens to the voice of God. Whether we understand His instructions or not, our job is to harken unto His voice and obey His instructions. As the scripture above states, there is nowhere to hide for those who turn their backs on God and ignore His warnings. On the other hand, those of us who are willing to obey His voice above all others, will experience the goodness of the Lord in the land of the living!

In my years of walking with God, I have learned the most beneficial position I'll ever experience is the posture of surrender. When I surrender my heart to the Lord and harken to his voice, I get the supreme joy of fellowship with Him. That is always the goal, intimate fellowship with the One who loved me first.

A surrendered heart harkens…

As He calls, I answer. As I answer, He transforms me.

Day 8
I Have an Assurance of Victory!

"Now thanks be to God who always leads us in triumph in Christ, and through us diffuses the fragrance of His knowledge in every place." -**II Corinthians 2:14 NKJV**

God, I thank you that I have an eternal assurance of victory. Even when it seems as though defeat is imminent, I take comfort in your word. I have a promise of victory. You knew before the worlds were formed that I would have days like this… days that I wondered how in the world I would make it through another battle. And in your infinite wisdom, you led me to this scripture so that I would have an anchor of truth to tether my mind to. Thank you, Jesus, for loving me so much that you sacrificed your life so that I would have an assurance of victory no matter how strong my opponent appears to be.

Holy Spirit, thank you for always speaking up within me, reminding me to wipe the tears from my eyes and trust the God of my salvation. The moment of battle; the time between the attack and the gathering of spoils is won when I remember that you will never allow a battle I cannot win. That means if it is here, victory is also here! Hallelujah to the Lamb of God that was slain before the foundations of the world, and thanks be unto God who always causes us to triumph!!!

Use the space below to write 10 victory confessions for your life.

Day 9
Why do you cry to me?

"But Moses told the people, "Don't be afraid. Just stand still and watch the Lord rescue you today. The Egyptians you see today will never be seen again. The Lord himself will fight for you. Just stay calm." Then the Lord said to Moses, "Why are you crying out to me? Tell the people to get moving!" -Exodus 14:13-15 NLT

Have you ever had a moment when you were in between a rock and a hard place and had no idea how you were going to get out of the situation? This is what was happening to the Israelites in the scripture above. They were standing in front of the Red Sea with the Egyptians closing in on them. Out of frustration and fear, they'd cried out to God and complained to Moses that it would have been better for them to remain slaves in Egypt.

In that moment, the Israelites forgot it was their pleas for help that caused God to send Moses to them. They forgot about the plagues God had spared them from before they left Egypt and most importantly, they forgot God has already promised to lead them to the promised land.

I used to wonder how they could forget such pivotal moves of God. Until one day, I found myself standing in between a rock and a hard place and felt my own panic creep into the pit of my belly. My entire life is a testament to the goodness and faithfulness of God, yet there I was standing in fear and frustration just like the Israelites.

Just like He did with the Israelites, God used my "hard" place to remind me of how faithful He is to keep His promises. He did not respond to my fear or frustration, instead, He reminded me there was no need to cry out to Him regarding a situation He'd already promised to deliver me out of.

I know God hears me every time I pray, but I also believe there comes a time when God will simply remind us to follow His instructions. In the scripture referenced above, it was like God was saying, "You don't have time to cry. Egyptians are behind you, and I already told you I would take care of you. Look at what you have in your hand and use it!"

This is your moment to review what you already have in your hand AND the instructions God has already given you. Nothing ever catches God by surprise so the situation you are facing already has a God-designed solution. Your job is to stop crying, wash your face, review the instructions God has already given you, and use what He placed in your hands to get to the other side of this situation.

Get up from your seat of sadness and move forward in victory!!!

What areas of your life have caused you to pause and tremble with fear? Have there been moments when the frustration was so great that you felt tempted to return to bondage and stagnation? After reading this entry, how has your perspective changed? What can you say to your future self so that fear and frustration will not hold you hostage?

_____
_____
_____
_____
_____
_____
_____
_____
_____

Otescia R. Johnson

Day 10
You Are Just the Vessel

I LOVE music with a beautiful message...regardless of genre. Years ago, I enjoyed the TV show Nashville, not just for the story line, but for the beautiful music that is showcased week after week. God often speaks to me through music and even more so through the story behind the music. Once particular song from Nashville, stuck out to me. It is called, *It Ain't Yours to Throw Away*. The part of this song that grabbed me was, "*What if you're just a vessel and God gave you something special? It ain't yours to throw away. It ain't yours to throw away. Every time you open up your mouth, diamonds come rolling out, It ain't yours to throw away...*" You can find the full song on YouTube, but I want to share why this song stopped me in my tracks the first time I heard it.

Have you ever wanted to give up in the face of adversity? Have you ever had a moment so tough that it caused you to rethink everything you believed about yourself? Have you ever been told to stop dreaming about making it big and get a real job? Have you ever felt like what you are destined to do may just be too big for you to handle?

When those moments of attempted destiny homicide arise, remember this, you're just the vessel... it's not yours to throw away!!!

Get up, dust yourself off, take up your cross and move towards your destiny! How can you give up on (throw away) something that is not even really yours?!?!? YOU ARE JUST THE VESSEL! The wineskin doesn't say it can no longer hold the wine, right? How then can you say you cannot carry something that you were created to hold until the appointed time and then release into the atmosphere!?

That's what we are all created to do...hold, guard, nurture, and protect our perspective destinies until the appointed time. When that time arises, we MUST release that which we have carried! Just as in a natural pregnancy the final month is often the most uncomfortable. Expectant mothers are often anxious to give birth if for no other reason, they are excited to see their baby. Imagine the outrage at a mother that decides to "throw her baby away" in the 9th month! That's the equivalent of what we do when we throw away the seeds God plants inside of us when life gets difficult. Those seeds are precious and needed to impact this world! While we are the vessels, what is inside of us do not belong to us and therefore are not ours to throw away!

What have you been sitting on that you have been tempted to throw away? Take a moment to set an atmosphere of worship, then use the space below to converse with God about what you have been chosen to carry and birth into the earth.

Day 11
Know the Members of Your Herd!

"For where two or three are gathered together in my name, there am I in the midst of them." -**Matthew 18:20**

One day while absently flipping through the television channels I came across a show on the National Geographic channel. This particular special followed the hunting patterns of hyenas. Due to a decrease in their food supply, the pack of hyenas was forced to hunt close to a pride of lions. Night after night the hyenas came up empty handed because the lions were hunting in close groups and dominating any prey they came across. Often times the hyenas would sit on the side lines waiting for the lions to slip up just once so they could get a taste of the prey. After nights of waiting, the perfect opportunity came for the hyenas. A lioness had wandered away from the pride in search of food. She found an animal, quickly killed it, and began to eat her dinner. Just as quickly as she had taken down the animal, a pack of hyenas swarmed her and wrestled her kill away from her. Knowing she was outnumbered, the lioness retreated with little resistance.

While watching this, the Spirit of the Lord spoke to me, "See that's exactly how Satan works. When you are with your fellow sisters and brothers in Christ you are strengthened, so he tries to isolate you so he can devour you!" {Be sober, be vigilant; because your adversary the devil, as a roaring lion, walketh about, seeking whom he may devour ~ 1 Peter 5:8} Do not be fooled by this trick of the enemy. There is always safety in numbers! When you feel hard pressed on every side, run to Jesus and ask Him to reveal to you the members of your herd for that situation. While we recognize Jesus is our source for all we need, we also recognize that He often works through people He places in our paths. When you come together with the members of you herd; the herd God has joined together for your edification, you will find safety! When the herd comes together (Matthew 18:20), Jesus is there in the midst of them! The hyena (satan) knows better than to attack the entire herd, because he is defenseless against Jesus!

It is imperative that we as believers recognize our "herd" and stick together. Just as the hyenas preyed on an animal they would otherwise be afraid of when they saw an open opportunity, so does the devil attempt to prey on us when we do not seek support from one another. We then that are strong ought to bear the infirmities of the weak, and not to please ourselves. ~Romans 15:1 Today I may be strong and you weak, but next week the roles may be reversed and I may need you to bear my infirmities. If I pull away from you during my "weak" season and try to "handle" things alone one of us would be lacking in either giving or receiving support. I know there will be times when the Lord will instruct us to speak to Him alone regarding the issues of life, but even then, know He has placed you on the heart and mind of someone in the herd and they are bearing you up in prayer. Know your herd (not necessarily members of your local church body, but often times will be), love your herd (love with the love of Christ, not from your emotions), run with your herd (stick with the people God leads you to stick with)!

It is also important for us to remember in our "strong" seasons not to forget about the weak. God does not strengthen us just for us. He strengthens us that we may strengthen others. In Luke 22:31-32 Jesus said, "Simon, Simon, behold, satan hath desired to have you, that he may sift you as wheat. But I have prayed for thee, that thy faith fail not; and when thou art converted strengthen they brethren." When you are experiencing your mountain top, do not forget about your herd members who are still in the valley. Carry the burden of prayer for them (as the Holy Spirit leads) until they see victory or until the burden lifts. In all things, be led of the Spirit of God!

Day 12
I Fell in Love in a Closet

God, I will never forget the tiny two-bedroom apartment that solidified my relationship with you. You and I both know that apartment held some of the most painful memories of my 20's, but on the floor of that closet when I laid down and let the prayers stream from my eyes as tears, you were right there to comfort me. Putting the kids down for their nap and meeting you in that closet made the difference between me fighting for my life and me giving up. I thought I knew you before that season of my life, but I was sure I loved you and you loved me after that season.

When I think of my life, I often attribute who I am to those hours of laying on the floor of that closet. It's where I realized You were pulling me into a deeply abiding love affair with You. It's where the scales began to fall from my eyes and what I thought I knew of love was shattered so that truth could be built in its place. That narrow, walk-through closet was the birthplace of my love affair with You, but now, more than 20 years later, I realize Your love affair with me began long before You formed me in my mother's womb.

I fell in love in a closet, but You loved me long before I knew how to love myself or recognize the unconditional perfect love of a Heavenly Father. Thank You for loving me so deeply and meeting me during the darkest moments of my life. Thank You for rescuing my mind even when I wasn't sure I wanted to be rescued. Thank You for filling in the gaps for me when I couldn't even form words to pray. Thank You for never giving up on me and loving all of my, even in my brokenness, until I could honestly say, I love you too.

I fell in love in a closet…

Use the space below to recount your own love story with God. Where did you fall in love with Him?

_____
_____
_____
_____
_____
_____
_____
_____
_____

Forever His

Day 13
Worship Part 2

"Then I said, "Behold, I come; in the scroll of the book it is written of me. I delight to do Your will, O my God, and Your law is within my heart." -Psalms 40:7-8 NKJV

There is a song by Moses Akoh (*Volume of the Book*) that is based on the scripture above. Every time I hear the song, it sends me into worship. It always reminds me of the intimate conversations God and I have behind closed doors. It is an echo of the cry of my heart.

Take a few moments to listen to the song for yourself and use the space below to journal what you hear in your spirit.

_____
_____
_____
_____
_____
_____

Forever His

Day 14
A Lifestyle of Prayer and Fasting

So often, we view prayer and fasting as arduous work. There's nothing that sounds fun or entertaining about denying your body the things it desires. Yet, prayer and fasting are two of the most powerful weapons in the arsenal of the Believer. When we develop a lifestyle of prayer and fasting, not by religious ritual, but out of devotion to our God, this lifestyle prepares us for any and every attack we will face.

The Bible says in Matthew 17:21 (AMP), "[But this kind of demon does not go out except by prayer and fasting.]" So often we try to begin fasting and praying when the attack materializes, but the truth is we need to stay ready, so we don't have to get ready. One should not wait until a demonic spirit reveals itself to begin praying and fasting. In this passage of scripture, the disciples had attempted to cast out a demon but were unsuccessful. When they asked Jesus why they were unsuccessful, He responded by first telling them they were operating in unbelief. Then He went on to basically say the only way to have enough strength and power to cast out this type of demonic spirit is to live a lifestyle of prayer and fasting.

Prayer is not something we only do in perilous times. Prayer is the life force for those who live in fellowship with God! Can you imagine having a friend or close loved one that you only speak to when things are going wrong? Would you really believe that person was your friend or that they love you? No! You'd start to wonder how much they actually cared about you because they don't make time to speak with you. This is what it is like to be in relationship with God. Because He loves us, He wants to talk to us often. If we love Him, the same should be true for us!

Prayer is a perfected form of two-way communication. It's not only a time for us to share what is on our hearts with God, but it gives God permission to share what is on His heart. When we grow in our fellowship with the Father, He begins to share His mysteries and the things that please and grieve Him with us. The deeper we go in God, the deeper our communion with Him becomes.

Then, as we develop the lifestyle of prayer, we begin to hear God's instruction to fast. Fasting silences the voice of our fleshly desires so that we can hear our spirit more clearly. The Bible teaches us in Galatians 5:17 that our flesh and spirit are at war daily. The only way to ensure the spirit wins the battle over the flesh, is to starve the flesh and feed the spirit. When you heed God's instruction to fast, you starve the flesh and strengthen your spirit. This is what empowers us to always be ready for battle. Again, our lifestyle enables us to stay ready so we'll never have to worry about getting ready! When you develop the lifestyle of prayer and fasting, you will always be battle ready because prayer gives us insight to discern what is ahead, and fasting strengthens and equips our spirit for battle!

Make this your confession, I am not a reactive Christian! I am a proactive Christian!

Day 15
God's Decree

"Yes indeed, it won't be long now." God's Decree. "Things are going to happen so fast your head will swim, one thing fast on the heels of the other. You won't be able to keep up. Everything will be happening at once—and everywhere you look, blessings! Blessings like wine pouring off the mountains and hills. I'll make everything right again for my people Israel: "They'll rebuild their ruined cities. They'll plant vineyards and drink good wine. They'll work their gardens and eat fresh vegetables. And I'll plant them, plant them on their own land. They'll never again be uprooted from the land I've given them.", your God, says so." -**Amos 9:13-15 (MSG)**

Yes indeed!!!! It won't be long now!!! This passage of scripture is so powerful for those who feel as though their victory has been delayed. Sometimes, delay can happen simply because we have an expectation of a future turn around as opposed to trusting God to be the God of Amos 9:13, right NOW! When you pray as though things are a far off, you literally set yourself up for disappointment. The Bible tells us that NOW faith is the subject of things hoped for and the evidence of things not seen. (Hebrews 11:1) When you pray as though

God's answers are not already YES and AMEN, you delay the manifestation of what you are praying for. Amos reminds us to bring our faith into the now!

Yes indeed… it won't be long now!

Doesn't that increase your excitement?!? This isn't something you are going to have to pray and wait for! The time for things to happen so fast it makes your head swim is NOW!!!

Read Amos 9:13-15 MSG again. Use the space below to write out the decrees God has spoken to you.

_____
_____
_____
_____
_____
_____
_____
_____
_____
_____
_____

Forever His

Day 16
Write Everything He Gives You

"Otescia. I have my good book tremble going on! I felt so many emotions! I caught myself smiling and making shock and awe sounds while reading. Currently, I feel sad b/c of reading Reese's situation, but a part of me is wondering if she is not telling him b/c she doesn't want to miscarry and have him deal with it in a war zone. Now looka here... we are gonna need this book in print ASAP! Btw...within the last few years...only Carl Weber has been talented enough to give me my readers tremble... so in other words... I LOVE IT!"

The quoted message above was sent to me on 4/10/13 by a dear friend who has now transitioned to be with the Lord, Kristie Lynn Cooks. I was writing my very first fiction book and felt super nervous about whether or not it would be "good enough". I sent Kristie a few chapters to read and review as I was writing, and the message above was her response.

Over the years, Kristie became one of the biggest encouragers to my writing journey. When I would secretly doubt the story line I was envisioning, Kristie would have a dream about me, my books, or my movies. God used her to teach me very valuable lesson: Everything I create flows from a heart that loves God, therefore He will be a part of everything I create!

When religious strongholds tried to keep me bound, I'd remember one of Kristie's dreams about being at my movie premiere. When I begged God to give me Christian characters so my books would be received well by Christians, I'd remember Kristie telling me my books would be compared to the likes of John Grisham. (This happened in 2016 by the way.) When I worried I did not have the creative chops and discipline to write a 70k word novel, Kristie would message me and tell me how she wasn't able to put the chapters I sent her down. She was God's messenger to help encourage me on a journey that changed my life forever!

"Write everything He gives you," became a statement I've learned to recite to myself when doubt tries to make me water down the story I see in my mind's eye. The dozens of messages I have from my friend played a major part in building my confidence to live this statement. My question to you is, what have you watered down out of fear of being judged, or being worried you were not good enough to accomplish the task in front of you? Where have you made yourself small out of fear you did not have what it takes to accomplish such a major goal?

Otescia R. Johnson

In the space below, articulate the areas God is nudging you to trust Him, believe in yourself, and go bigger than you ever thought you could!

Day 17
He desires to give you your heart's desires!

"Trust in the Lord, and do good; Dwell in the land, and feed on His faithfulness. Delight yourself also in the Lord, and He shall give you the desires of your heart. Commit your way to the Lord, trust also in Him, and He shall bring it to pass." **Psalms 37:3-5 (NKJV)**

I always read this scripture assuming it meant God would give me the things I desired because I never read it in full context. I always started and stopped with He would give me the desires of my heart. Then, one day as I was working on a project, He opened the scripture to me in a new way. I read the three verses above, and it hit me… Yes, God wants to give the things I desire, but that's because He was the One who planted the seed of desire inside of me.

As I trust in God and live uprightly before Him, He plants the seed of desire within my heart. Then, as I commit myself and my ways to Him and trust Him, He brings that desire to pass. When I studied the word delight, I learned it means to be soft or tender. So, as I soften my heart towards God, He responds to that tenderness by sowing seeds of desire within the garden of my heart. Then, as I continue with my intimate walk with Him, He causes the very thing He planted within me to come to pass!!!

As I grow in my understanding and revelation of the passage above, I realize, when God spoke through the Prophet Jeremiah and said, "I know the plans *and* thoughts that I have for you,' says the Lord, 'plans for peace *and* well-being and not for disaster, to give you a future and a hope," He was revealing to us that He's been intentional about us all along. Mankind is the only form of creation that was given free will. God will never go against our will. Therefore, He created a pathway to ensure what we desire is in alignment with the plans He has for our lives. Now we enter into the divine order of Psalms 37:3-5. When we delight ourselves in the Lord, we activate the pathway for God's future and hope for us to come to pass!

Father,

I thank you that my love for you and intimate communion with you is always producing the fruit of the seeds you sow within me. My heart safely trusts in You and You alone. Thank you for opening your scriptures up to me so that I can grow deeper in my understanding and revelation of your plan for my life. I have spent so much time attempting to purge my heart of desires I thought came from my own will, but You have revealed to me the thing I tried to shake off was actually Your will for me because You gave me that desire and, in Your timing, You will bring it to pass.

Who am I that You are so mindful of me… that You were so intentional about me and the things You have ordained for my life. When I couldn't see past the pain of the day, you were pulling me into an even deeper relationship with you because you knew this relationship would give birth to every good and perfect thing You have planned for me.

I love you and I pray my lifestyle is always conducive for You to give me the desires of my heart which are the seeds of the plans you have for me!

Your daughter,
Otescia

In the space below, start a dialogue with God about His will for your life, your desires, and how the two intersect. Remember He knew you before He formed you in your mother's womb, so your true desires can't be hidden from Him. Be transparent with Him so that He can bring you into perfect alignment with His will!

_____
_____
_____
_____
_____
_____
_____
_____
_____
_____
_____
_____
_____
_____
_____
_____

Forever His

Day 18
Thank You for my Husband

God, I never knew You loved me so deeply, so unconditionally, until you sent Lyndell into my life. I marvel at how something so completely clear to me now could have been hidden from my sight for so long. Thank you for loving me so much that you sent ANOTHER human to Earth as an embodiment of your love for me. Jesus was first, but in my limited understanding of love, I did not grasp the depth of what it meant for You to love me unconditionally. To have another human see me at my absolute worst, to see me broke and broken and choose to pick me up, cradle me in his arms and love me until I can love myself again… Wow God! You've blown me away by your never-ending desire to reveal your love to me.

May I always love, honor, and respect the gift You've given to me in Lyndell. Help me to remember his example of love and in return love him unconditionally. Thank you, Lord, for maturing the romantic love I have with my husband while simultaneously deepening the agape love I experience with You. What an absolute honor it is to experience supernatural and natural love simply because it was Your design for me all along. When I cried out to you in despair, feeling lonely and unloved, You revealed I was loved more than I ever imagined. I am forever grateful.

Love always,
Otescia

Use the space below to write your unconditional love story. It can be your love story with God or another person.

_____
_____
_____
_____
_____
_____
_____
_____
_____
_____
_____

Otescia R. Johnson

Day 19
Watch YOUR Mouth

"Run away from infantile indulgence. Run after mature righteousness—faith, love, peace—joining those who are in honest and serious prayer before God. Refuse to get involved in inane discussions; they always end up in fights. God's servant must not be argumentative, but a gentle listener and a teacher who keeps cool, working firmly but patiently with those who refuse to obey. You never know how or when God might sober them up with a change of heart and a turning to the truth, enabling them to escape the Devil's trap, where they are caught and held captive, forced to run his errands." - **2 Timothy 2:22-26 (MSG)**

For those who may not know, I was married previously. 2.5 months before my 18th birthday, I entered into a marriage that was not ordained by God. As a result, my early 20s were very, very painful years for me. After that divorce, I decided being divorced meant I never had to argue again. I refused to go into another marriage filled with those types of emotions. Even though I said those things to myself, it took the Lord stepping in and speaking directly to me for me to really get it!

God brought the most gentle, supportive, and loving soul into my life, my husband Lyndell.

When the Lord revealed to me that Lyndell was my husband He also said, "He will not tolerate your mouth." I was thrown off by this because I thought I was doing great. I'd never even been upset with Lyndell, so I hadn't said anything wrong to him. That was God's point though. He was revealing to me the area I needed to work on before the marriage so that I would not cause needless problems in the future.

It's one thing for a person to demand your respect, it's another when the Lord tells you to give it! Because let's face it, speaking to each other properly is a form of respect. I must confess this has been an easier area for me to watch my mouth because my husband ALWAYS speaks to me out of love and respect.

The hard part for me was learning to speak to others with respect even when they do not do so with me. The scripture did not say only refrain from arguments when the other person is nice to you! We must always conduct ourselves according to this passage no matter how rude or impolite the other person is. I will be the first person to confess I don't always pass the test, but I continue trying and with God's help I am getting much better.

When the Lord spoke to me about Lyndell I had no idea the above scripture even existed. When I came across the scripture one day in my personal study time, I realized this not arguing thing went well beyond my marriage. It's His will for us to be "a gentle listener and a teacher that keeps our cool"! That means even though you may be right, there is still a correct way to present what you are trying to teach the other person. Who listens when they are being belittled, yelled at, or ridiculed? Instead of listening to what you are saying (teaching), they go on the defense and now neither of you are listening!

Another thing to remember is, you are a living witness! Everything you say and do reflects your walk with Christ. Arguing with people affects your witness. Will they hear you when you try to share the love of God if you just cussed them out yesterday? Will the unbelieving spouse come to Jesus if you are constantly yelling and fussing? Can you pass the test of not being argumentative? Is it more important for you to express your emotions, or for you to show Jesus to a dying world?!?!

We have to become better at showing His presence on the inside of us. We are His ambassadors here in the earth. When people see us, they should also see the love of Jesus. If we are arguing, Jesus is not being seen in us. Together, we can change this world! We can make a difference in the lives of those that are lost, but it starts with watching what we say and how we say it!

Read 2 Timothy 2:22-26 (MSG) again. Take a few moments to mediate on the passage. Write what you sense, see, hear, and feel below.

Day 20
Think on These Things

"Finally, brethren, whatever things are true, whatever things are noble, whatever things are just, whatever things are pure, whatever things are lovely, whatever things are of good report, if there is any virtue and if there is anything praiseworthy—meditate on these things."

-Philippians 4:8 (NKJV)

Like many of the character-shifting "ah-ha" moments of my life, I was in my early 20's when the scripture above resonated with me. My pastor at the time gave us an assignment to memorize and meditate on the verse. I don't think I ever memorized it correctly, but the message stuck with me forever. There are things we are supposed to be thinking about and things we should avoid thinking about.

The mind is such a powerful part of our existence. It is the control center that dictates all of our bodily functions. How we think controls how we feel, which plays an important role in our actions. If we desire to change our actions, we must first change our thoughts. I challenge you to spend a few days meditating on this scripture.

Afterwards, use the space below to journal your experience.

Day 21
I Miss My Brother

The entry below is one of the most vulnerable of this book. If you are experiencing the highs and lows of mourning the loss of a loved one, I pray you are strengthened and encouraged by my journey.

> *"God, you have to give me something to anchor my mind to. I won't make it if you don't."*

I was sitting in the hospital room looking at my brother's lifeless body. He was supposed to have surgery to clean a wound the following morning, but he never made it. He died shortly after he and I spoke on the phone that night.

"He defied the odds." That's the phrase that popped into my mind. God comforted my heart in that moment and reminded me my brother was given a death sentence while my mother was carrying him. She was told countless times he wouldn't live past a certain age. Then, when he surpassed the medical teams' expectations, they said he would never walk or talk. He did both of those things and even started several businesses. He defied the odds.

In that cold hospital room, God immediately answered my request and gave me a word that would anchor my thoughts. In the days that followed, tormenting thoughts came to me

> Why didn't you just push past the fatigue and come see him today?

> Why were you so afraid of walking in the parking garage alone at night?

> How can you see everything else, but missed this?

> God!!! Why didn't you show me his life was on the line?

As I planned my brother's memorial service, all of those thoughts swirled through my mind. But each time I thought the fear and grief would overtake me, a superimposing thought would prevail. He defied the odds. God kept rescuing my mind so that I would not be consumed or swallowed up by sadness.

It took me months of processing the sadness of losing my brother for me to put all these pieces together. I will miss my brother for as long as I live. However, I never folded into grief and depression because when I asked God to help me, He immediately reminded me that I had 36 years of memories to be grateful for. While I will always want more time with my brother on Earth, I recognize his entire life was God keeping a promise to my mother.

When I think of my brother's unexpected passing now, I also think of God rescuing my mind. I now know God as my personal rescuer. He swooped in and helped stabilize my mind and heart because I turned to Him when my heart was breaking inside of my chest. Before grief could stick its claws in me, God rescued me! I mourned. I did not grieve as the world describes grief. I mourned his presence yet chose not to listen to or sit in negative emotions. I felt what I felt and gave myself permission to be sad and grateful simultaneously.

Over the years the sadness has faded, but make no mistake, I still miss my brother. I miss his boisterous laugh. I miss being called his little big sister. I miss the way he showed up for the important moments in my children's lives. I miss his smile that lit up the room. And above all else, I miss reminiscing about our childhood shenanigans with him. I will always miss him, but I will forever be grateful to God for rescuing my mind and teaching me how to remain mentally healthy even in mourning.

Otescia R. Johnson

I shared a portion of my story of loss, mourning, and continuing to live without the physical presence of a loved one. Have you lost someone you still miss? If so, please use the space below to write your story.

Forever His

Day 22

A Loving Father

"All you lovers of God who want to please him, come and listen, and I'll tell you what he did for me. I cried aloud to him with all my heart, and he answered me! Now my mouth overflows with the highest praise. Yet if I had closed my eyes to my sin, the Lord God would have closed his ears to my prayer. But praises rise to God, for he paid attention to my prayer and answered my cry to him! I will forever praise this God who didn't close his heart when I prayed and never said no when I asked him for help. He never once refused to show me his tender love."

-Psalms 66:16-20 (TPT)

He never once refused to show me His tender love… the latter part of the passage above moves my heart to tears. God, in His unfailing love for me, chooses to hear my prayers and respond to my cry. Our God, ruler of all of Heaven and Earth, the Master of the whole Universe, is sensitive to sound of our voices! What a kind, loving, and faithful Father we serve!!!

When the cares of life are heavy and threatening to interfere with our faith, the passage above is a reminder to seek out the help of the Father. If the situation you are facing was caused by poor decision making or sin, God's only requirement is repentance and an invitation to step in.

Have you ever found yourself in a situation of your own making and looked up to God for help out of sheer desperation? I have, but if I'm totally transparent, shame and guilt initially prevented me from coming to God for help. I felt I got myself into the situation, so it was my responsibility to get myself out. Nothing could have been further from the truth. God already had a solution for me. When I went to Him, repented, and asked for help, like in the passage above, God quickly heard my prayer and responded with His solution. He came to my rescue!

This is why I can now say when I cried out to Him in my day of trouble, He answered me! I can say this without shame, because through that situation, God proved to me that He would always show up when I call Him. As long as I'm breathing, I have an opportunity to repent and turn to Him. In truth, that's all He really wants from His children. He doesn't desire to punish us. He longs to save us. He longs to save us so much, that He sent His son to do so. What a forgiving and loving Father we serve!

Day 23

He Leads Me to His Best

"He restoreth my soul: he leadeth me in the paths of righteousness for his name's sake" **- Psalm 23:3**

Have you ever wanted something so badly that the idea of God not doing it for you never even entered into your mind? Have you ever prayed, fasted, and stepped out on faith only to have the door slammed in your face? Well, I have, and let me be the first to acknowledge this one truth everyone seems to shy away from...IT HURTS! It hurts when you feel like God did not give you the one thing you so earnestly desired. But allow me to let you in on one little secret; if God shuts a door, He does it so that He can point you in the direction of another one. He blocks door number one because while what lay behind the door may *seem* like it's good for you, He knows this door is not **His BEST** for you! His ultimate desire is for you to walk in His perfect will and experience His very best in every area of your life!!!

We often think of God leading us as Him speaking every direction into our spirit, but sometimes His leading comes in the form of a denial. He didn't allow you to get the $15/hour job, because he knew He had already prepared the $30/hour position. Your first record contract fell through because He knew the record label was filled with crooks and thieves! Your first business failed because God saw the direction you were headed in was not His plan for your future. Even in God's denial or blockage of what appears right in our own eyes, He is leading us to the prepared place which contains the blessings He has stored up for us!

It's easy to recognize His leading when it comes in a way you can understand, so let's start by understanding this...in all things God is leading you towards the path that was designed for your greater good. He loves you and desires to see you whole and complete. Instead of shedding tears when the next door slams shut in your face, understand that is God's way of letting you know that door was not His best for you! I am learning to stop crying over closed doors that are at best sub-par, and start looking for the doors that God is trying to lead me to! In all things, He leads me!

This is not an easy process because it requires a re-programming of my brain. It requires a consist reminder that the pain and disappointment that often accompanies a closed door is a humanistic reaction to a spiritual decision. We know God's ways are not our ways, yet we often expect Him to prepare things the way we would prepare them. When we want to teach our children a lesson, we often sit them down and talk to them. We express what we want them to learn and expect them to just "get it". God, however, understands that in order to truly learn a lesson there must be some sort of application of the knowledge gained. This means when you hear a word from God concerning your future, there has to be some sort of corresponding action to put that word into practice.

When it is time to begin making the steps towards positioning ourselves to receive what it is that God has spoken, we try to act based on how we "think" the plan should go. We often forget His ways are not our ways. So instead of rejoicing when He leads us by closing all of the wrong doors, we listen to the negative thoughts and ideas presented by our limited humanistic understanding rather than relying on the truth of His word! Instead of rejoicing at the closed door, which by the way is a beautiful example of the process of elimination, we become sad and disappointed.

I am attempting to grow into a place of maturity that will enable me to recognize the closed doors as a sign of God's process of elimination. When the wrong doors are closed around me, eventually I will be left with the right door! As this lesson is learned (through practical application) I will then be ready for God to simply point to the door, and I walk right through it!

If you are tired of the emotional roller coaster that comes along with closed doors, I encourage you to go to God and ask Him to give you personal revelation of how and where He is leading you. In all things, His desire is for your best life here in the earth and after you take your final breath. Following His leading even in the painful places, puts you in a position to live as He originally intended...perfect and complete, lacking nothing!!! Stay in the process. The closed doors do not feel great, but eventually you will learn how to be guided to the right door the first time around!

In the space below, start a conversation with God about doors He has closed for you and the doors He is leading you to walk through.

_____

_____

_____

_____

_____

_____

Otescia R. Johnson

Day 24

Worship Part 3

*L**ord You Are Good* by Todd Galberth is one of my go-to surrender songs. It always reminds me that no matter how difficult life may become, I have a loving Father who is working behind the scenes and causing all things to work together for my good. (Romans 8:29)

Take a few moments to listen to the song for yourself and use the space below to journal what you hear in your spirit.

_____

_____

_____

_____

_____

_____

Otescia R. Johnson

Day 25

Come See a Man

The story of how we all came to know Jesus, while, different in detail, is mostly identical in nature. A broken, wounded, and lost individual encountered a perfect Savior who knew everything about our past and chose to love us anyway. I can't think of a better illustration of the salvation story than the story of the Samaritan woman at the well. Her story is found in John chapter 4. I won't share the exact scripture here. Instead, I'm going to retell the story in modern vernacular. Feel free to read the actual biblical account in your study time.

Here we go…

Jesus was on his way to Galilee, but He had to stop in Samaria. While He was there, His disciples left Him alone at a well while they went to go find food. As He sat there alone, a woman approached the well. Now, Jesus was fully

God and fully man at the same time, so when he saw this woman, He instantly knew everything about her. He knew she had a "high body count". For those who may not know what that means, Sis had her pick of men from the village, gave them all a ride on her carousel, but none of them married her. Even still, Jesus saw this lady drawing water from the well and was like, "Aye, while you're getting your water, go ahead and grab some for me."

Now, Sis knew there was a big difference between her and Jesus. He was a Jew, and she was a Samaritan, so she confronted Him on asking her for water. In my mind, she was confused but also had a bit of an attitude. She was probably thinking she was tired of men asking her for stuff. I mean think about it, if she'd been from man to man but none of them married her, there had to be some sort of built-up resentment or frustration. But instead of really popping off at the mouth, she said, "I'm a Samaritan and you're a Jew. Why would you ask me for water?"

Jesus then spit that Holy knowledge to her and was like, "If you knew about this water I'm offering, you would be asking me for water instead of the other way around. This water I have is living water and those who drink it don't ever get thirsty again!" After hearing that, Sis changed her tune. She wanted that water because she was tired of being thirsty. I like to think of this as being deeper than her mouth being parched. I believe this woman was tired of the thirst in her soul and the idea of the water Jesus was offering was REFRESHING!

Jesus, being the wise and skilled Evangelist that He is, used this as an opportunity to get to the root of the woman's issue. In response to her request for water, Jesus told her to go get her husband. Remember He was fully God and fully man, so He knew what her answer would be, but Jesus was working on something. When the woman confessed, she did not have a husband, Jesus basically read her like a book and told her, *"You're right! You don't have a husband— for you have had five husbands, and you aren't even married to the man you're living with now. You certainly spoke the truth!"* (John 4:17b-18 NLT)

Now, I don't know about you reader, but if a stranger read me like that, I'm fairly certain I would not respond like this woman. I'm not sure how I would respond, but it wouldn't have been like her. Sis said, "You must be a prophet." (John 4:19 NLT) Now her next words threw me for a loop because instead of going back to that water Jesus told her about, Sis tried to start a theological debate. I believe this account was kept on the record so we would have an example to follow when evangelizing to unbelievers.

Jesus did not allow her to distract him by answering the question she asked. Instead, He stuck to His own script…the WORD! Jesus expertly redirected the conversation and kept the main thing, the main thing. This is a perfect example of how we should handle weird off-topic questions posed to us on social media, at family gatherings, at work, etc. Keep the conversations centered on Jesus and the commonalities of our experiences with Him. That's how we will win souls. Allowing the conversation to drift to our differences only opens the door for dissension and strife.

Now, still not 100% ready to just concede to Jesus, the woman tried the next trick in the "I know stuff too" play book. She told Jesus she knew the Messiah was coming and when He came, He would explain everything. She was playing right into Jesus' hand and didn't even know it! Jesus told her, "I Am the Messiah." (John 4:26 NLT)

Then the disciples showed up all confused about why Jesus was talking to the woman, but they weren't brave enough to ask Him. The woman didn't even bother responding to Jesus' proclamation, she just left her water jar and ran back to the village. Sis was telling everyone that was listening, "Y'all gotta come see this man! He told me everything I ever did. Y'all think he the Messiah?" And she must have been convincing because we know she had to have had a lil reputation around the village. You know how it is in small towns. Everybody knows everybody's business. So, you know they knew Sis had a high body count, but instead of judging the source, they listened to the message! (Wait a minute… that'll preach!)

The woman that was probably voted least likely to succeed in high school became the promoter for a spontaneous revival! The people all flocked to Jesus and begged Him to say there with them for a few days. Jesus stayed two days and the people of the village went from believing because of what the woman said, to believing because they heard Jesus for themselves! Her conversion story became a tool of mass salvation because she openly shared her encounter with Jesus without fear of being judged. She was so on fire after her conversion that she wanted to ensure others would be converted as well. The same passion that previously led her to ungodly things now led her to tell everyone who would listen to, "Come see a man!"

You see, the thing that kept you in bondage before Jesus, becomes a tool for Him to use once you surrender your life to Him. This woman had to have been attractive, passionate, or persuasive to attract so many men. We know this because Jesus told her, the man she LIVED with was not her husband. This means he didn't just stop by for sex. He stayed after the physical gratification was over. That meant she had something else to offer. I believe when Jesus saw her at the well, He was looking at that thing. That thing that drew men to her. Just as Jesus told the fishermen He would make them fishers of men, meaning He would take their natural kills and teach them how to use them spiritually, Jesus saw a skill in this woman. Yes, her knew of her sin, but He knew if she drank from His living water, the thirst that led her to misuse her gift would be satisfied.

Now the woman at the well has a new story. She's no longer the woman with the high body count misusing her gifts to quench her thirst. Now, she can be remembered as the woman who encountered Jesus at a well and ran to evangelize His message to everyone who would listen.

Do you remember your conversion story? When is the last time you shared it with anyone? Use the space below to write your conversion story.

_____
_____
_____
_____
_____
_____
_____
_____
_____
_____
_____

Forever His

Day 26

The God Who Reads My Tears

"You keep track of all my sorrows. You have collected all my tears in your bottle. You have recorded each one in your book."
-**Psalms 56:8 (NLT)**

Tears are liquid prayers. I don't know where I first heard this statement, but it has always brought me comfort. When I don't have the mental capacity to think of words to pray, the tears that roll down my cheeks are read by God. Just that thought brings tears to my eyes as I type this. Every tear I have ever shed has been captured and stored in Heaven! When I was alone on the floor of my closet, unsure if I wanted to continue living, God was right there collecting my tears in a bottle. Then, He took those tears, translated them, and recorded them in His book.

As a professional writer, this resonates deeply with me. I know the significance of each word I've chosen to include in every book I've written. Words are weighty to me. If I chose a specific word, it's because of the weight or value of that word. Since I am made in the image and likeness of God, I like to believe the same is true for Him. He weighs the words He writes in His book. Yet, my tears, the liquid words that streamed down my face were so incredibly valuable that God collected them and saw fit to include them in His book.

My heart swells with gratitude as this significant revelation washes over me. Though it felt as though I was all alone, anytime I shed a tear, I was the opposite of alone. I was being cared for by the greatest caretaker this world will ever know. My thoughts and feelings are so important to Him that he made sure not a single tear was left unaccounted for. Who wouldn't serve a God like this?!?

While I know we as humans could never do anything to earn the love and attention of God, I still sometimes wonder what in the world I could have done to get to live this life of intimate love and care with Him. The depths of my gratitude will never be adequately described or expressed, but I believe He knows. In fact, I am sure He does because He is the God who reads my tears, even the ones that fall as I marvel at His magnificence.

Think of what it means to have God collect and record your tears. Meditate on the care He must take to interpret and translate every single tear. Use the space below to write what you sense and feel.

_____
_____
_____
_____
_____
_____
_____
_____
_____
_____
_____
_____
_____
_____
_____
_____

Day 27

Prayer for My Sons

"For I will fight those who fight you, and I will save your children."

-Isaiah 49:25b (NLT)

Father, I thank you for the male children you have blessed us with. I thank you Lord that they are healthy, whole, and lack nothing. Thank you for captivating their hearts in their youth that they will be compelled to follow after your ways. I speak life over them and call them obedient to your word. I speak to the man inside of them and call him a man of good moral character with a heart that beats for you. I curse distraction and worldly pressure to behave in ways that do not bring you glory. Make them a light for their generation even now. Cause them to walk in front of their peers as leaders who lead according to your word.

Thank you, Lord, for showing their father and I how to parent each of them individually. Thank you for teaching us how to communicate effectively with them that our relationships will be strong. Father, I thank you for guiding us as we guide them into manhood. Thank you for showing us how to live as Godly examples before them so that they won't go outside of the home looking for love and acceptance. Keep our bond with them secure so that we will always maintain our rightful positions of influence in their lives. Father, seal their nature so that they will not burn with desire before their time. I thank you that their appetite will be for the wives you have ordained for them. Thank you, Lord, for covering their eye and ear gates now so that they will not enter into any relationships that alter their future. Thank you, Lord, for teaching them what it means to be a man who loves God first and His wife second. Father, I thank you for the honor of raising Kingdom men who walk after the spirit and not after their flesh. Help us, as their parents, to remain calm and always speak to them in a way that cuts through any lie the enemy will ever try to feed them. I thank you now Lord that they are successful in all that you have destined for them to do in Jesus' name!

Thank you, Lord, for giving them the courage to follow you even when they do not understand why you are telling them to do the unusual thing. Guide us as we teach them to use what you have placed on the inside of them. Help us to sharpen and correct them without breaking their spirits. Show us how to discipline them in a way that produces the fruit you have ordained for their lives. We lean into YOU every day as we walk out our role as their parents, for we know you know what is best for their lives. We trust you to draw them unto you as we lift you up in our home. We give you praise for their lives and the work that you have for their hands to do. In Jesus' name we pray, Amen!

In the space below write a prayer for a child, grandchild, niece, nephew, or godchild.

_____
_____
_____
_____
_____
_____
_____
_____
_____
_____
_____
_____

Day 28

For your Maker is Your Husband...

According to an on-line study done in 2006, the average American couple spends around $26,802 on their wedding. This average estimate does not include the honeymoon or rings. This cost has sky rocketed over the years as Americans have began seeking out more lavish weddings. Everyone is looking for the best of the best. Some even go as far as to take out loans to pay to make their day "special". I once heard Dr. Phil say, "We spend all this time and money preparing for the wedding, and we're not preparing for the marriage". From a natural standpoint this is often true. More often than not, we get so focused on our big day that we neglect to prepare for life afterwards, so when storms come (and trust me they do), we are blind-sided and unprepared. Today I want to talk to you about a marriage that will never blind-side you, and a husband that will never leave you nor forsake you!

Isaiah 54:5 says, *"For your maker is your husband, the Lord of hosts is His name; and your redeemer is the Holy One of Israel; He is called the God of the whole Earth."*

From the days of John the Baptist until now, mankind has been entering into a marriage with the eternal bridegroom Jesus Christ that costs them no money whatsoever. In fact, He allows you to trade your sin, heartache, shame, and pain, for life and life more abundantly!

To marry means to form an affinity with. Affinity means to become related to. Married means to dwell, to remain, to settle.

Jesus Christ, our Lord and Savior desires to form a relationship with us that will remain. He desires to dwell with us throughout eternity!

Revelation 19:7-8 reads, "Let us be glad and rejoice and give Him glory, for the marriage of the Lamb has come, and His wife has made herself ready. And to her it was granted to be arrayed in fine linen, clean and bright, for the linen is the righteous acts of the saints."

Praise God!!!! This wedding will cost me nothing, not even the cost of a dress, for my righteous acts are my fine linen! To live righteously means to live in a way that is just; to walk in proper judgment; and to be equitable or holy. This life is a perpetual preparation for our eternal wedding. And guess what, you even have a wedding planner.... the Holy Spirit. If we would only listen, the wedding planner of our souls will lead you in **all truth and righteousness**. He keeps us on the straight and narrow throughout this life so that we may behold our bridegroom face to face when this natural life is over! The Holy Spirit is our wedding planner, make-up artist, hairstylist, nail technician, dress maker, florist...... He is everything we need to prepare us for our "big day"!

God is calling for a renewed commitment to Him! He's calling for us to live righteously. If you are ready to answer the call, recite the following:

I, (insert your name here), take you Jesus, to be my Lord and Savior, to honor and serve from this day forward, when this walk is easy and when it is not so easy, whether I have financial abundance or just enough, whether I encounter sickness or if I live in health, no matter what comes or what goes, I love and devote myself to your service from this day forward, Amen.

Day 29

The Lord is My Provider

"And my God will liberally supply (fill until full) your every need according to His riches in glory in Christ Jesus." - **Philippians 4:19 (AMP)**

"Otescia, I will not fight you to provide for you."

I will never forget the day God said this to me. I was crying about a financially dry season and begging God to step in and intervene. I was physically exhausted from the up and down rollercoaster of financial surplus and drought. Then I heard the phrase above and began to weep even harder. God was telling me the reason I'd been in such up and down seasons with money was because I never allowed Him to be my provider. I quoted the scripture above, but every time a financial need arose, I jumped into "let me find a solution" mode.

As a result, I kept ending up in financial peril. Without realizing what I was doing, I'd started relying on my own understanding, worldly financial provision, and the sweat of my own brow. I wrongly believed I was responsible for my own financial wellbeing. When the truth was, God desired to be my provider. He desired for me to trust Him with my daily needs. He wanted to give me more than I knew to ask for, but it would require me to submit to His WAY of providing.

God is a God of process. He teaches through hands on learning. This means instead of just zapping me with the ability to allow Him to be my provider, He processed me out of being my own provider. The process was far from easy. I cried so many days, but every day, God showed up and kept His promise of provision. He showed me what it means to be provided for in every area of my life. He challenged me to depend on Him when everything looks impossible. In one particularly hard moment, when it seemed God's process was leading me to devastation, I worshipped Him and made a vow. "I'll never stop praising You… no matter how it looks. As long as I have breath in my body, I will praise You!" I said those words with tears streaming down my face and meant every single one. In a matter of days, the situation that seemed impossible was turned around in my favor. My confession was a sign to God that I trusted Him to be my provider AND my worship of Him was not predicated on good times. I'll worship Him forever because He is the lover of my soul. When I stopped focusing on my needs and started focusing on the One who provides for my needs, provision showed up in ways I never expected!

"And since we know he hears us when we make our requests, we also know that he will give us what we ask for." **-1 John 5:15 (NLT)**

You have a promise of provision. Don't forfeit the promise trying to provide for yourself. Ask Him for what you need and trust Him to provide it!

Use the space below to ask God for what you need. Be specific and remember, He longs to provide for you!

_____

_____

_____

_____

_____

_____

_____

_____

_____

_____

_____

_____

Forever His

Day 30

My heart safely trusts in God...

I am an avid supporter of journaling. I have consistently kept prayer journals since 2008. When my life on earth is over, I pray these journals will be a blueprint for my children. In the front of every journal, I write the following statement:

My heart safely trusts in You. My God and King, I make you the Lord of my life. Rest, rule, and abide in me, in Jesus's name, Amen!

I started making this confession so that my heart and mind remain in alignment with God's requirement for my life. I don't have to be perfect, but in order to maintain the relationship with God that I've spent my life developing, I must trust Him with ALL of me. I must make Him the Lord of my life even when I do not understand His instructions or the pain He allows me to experience. This is a non-negotiable for my life. Remaining "Forever His" means forever surrendering to Him, His will, and His way.

Consider your relationship with the Lord. Are you committed to trusting Him with your whole heart? Can you trust Him even in the areas where disappointment has shown up in the past? Are you submitted to His will AND His way?

Use the space below to journal your thoughts on your trust walk with God and your submission to His will and way.

_____
_____
_____
_____
_____
_____
_____
_____
_____
_____
_____
_____

Otescia R. Johnson

Day 31

A Poem from my Dreams...

I awakened from a dream at 9:55pm on December 12, 2023. I'd barely fallen asleep when I was jolted awake, I grabbed my phone and typed the framework that would eventually become the following poem. I decided to share this entry at the end of this devotional as a nod to every woman who wonders if anyone understands their struggle. God speaks to us in a myriad of ways and on this day, He spoke to me in a rhythmic pattern that I later turned into a poem. I pray this not only makes you feel seen and understood, but that it will also give you permission to allow Holy Spirit to speak to and through you in whatever creative manner He chooses. All creativity comes from God.

Hey woman, I see you.
Yes you. I! SEE! YOU!
And I have a message
JUST! FOR! YOU!

Stop trying to be and just show up
For when you truly show up you'll learn how to be.

Government corrupt, an entangled web

Otescia R. Johnson

Lonely kids wander alone and unfed.
Until they met YOU.
The source of life and nurture
Loving what didn't even come from your body
Because it's in your nature.

From the older woman to the younger,
I see you Mama.
Times is rough and going is tough
Yet you making it Mana.

I! SEE! YOU!

I often stop to wonder
Do you regret the wander,
The years of shed tears
Memories clouded by drugs and fears?
Does it still bother you?
The mistakes of your youth?
Does it bother you that kids you raised are seeking other truths?

Oh…. And I see you.
I didn't overlook you
Sitting there feeling square
Wondering why you never fit in a round hole
Feeling empty and ashamed of all you've done trying to feel whole.

Older woman in the back, I see you too!
Remember the younger woman
Give her your strength through hugs

Forever His

Give her your praise through words
Pressing in your mind like a gentle nudge

Nudge… the soft subtle push forward to help you let go of that grudge.

Maybe from the younger you learn,
The art of letting go
A heart and mind so innocent,
Free from bloated inflated egos.

Woman to woman
I! SEE! YOU!
I understand you!
I feel you!
I know you!
Because I am you.

Woman to woman, I! SEE! YOU!

More books by Otescia R. Johnson

I Am Who I Am… & I'm Finally Cool with Her

Goodbye Egypt

Forever His

God Says I Am

Surviving the Sift

www.ingramcontent.com/pod-product-compliance
Lightning Source LLC
Chambersburg PA
CBHW050241010526
44107CB00040B/1473/J